I AM A FACE
SYMPATHIZING
WITH YOUR GRIEF

I AM A FACE
SYMPATHIZING
WITH YOUR GRIEF

Seven Younger Iranian Poets
Edited and Translated by Alireza Taheri Araghi

co·im·press

normal, illinois

Translation Copyright © 2015 by Alireza Taheri Araghi

Published by co•im•press
Normal, Illinois
www.coimpress.com

Printed by BookMobile

Distributed to the trade by Small Press Distribution
1341 Seventh Street, Berkeley, CA 94710
www.spdbooks.org

Cover and Book Design by co•im•press
Cover Image by Golnaz Shahmirzadi

First Edition 2015

ISBN: 978-0-9888199-5-5

Contents

Introduction

POETRY HAS long been an inseparable part of life in Iran. Rhythmic and rhymed classical forms, easier to memorize than prose, functioned as a versatile medium for passing down knowledge, telling stories, teaching grammar, and conveying messages, as well as, of course, expressing feelings. As a kid, before drastic social changes altered, and sometimes terminated, the more traditional ways of life (at least in the parts of the capital where I lived), I went to the neighborhood bath/shower house a few times. I remember two lines of poetry on the wall, above the man at the front desk, that read, "Confide to us any valuables you might have on you upon entering. We would not take responsibility for any lost items." Although poetry in Iran has almost ceased to function as a medium for legal disclaimers, it is still a highly esteemed literary form. The second most popular book in Iran (after the Quran) is probably the collection of sonnets by Hafez, a fourteenth-century Persian poet whose poems are still recited and memorized by many and published in the thousands by numerous presses all across the country. If you get engaged in a talk with the old owner of your neighborhood grocery store, you might hear him recite a few lines of "Heydar Baba," a long poem by the most famous Azeri poet, Mohammad-Hossein Shahriar. It wouldn't even be surprising to come across poetry as Facebook comments.

Around a hundred years ago, before Nima Yooshij wrote what is deemed by many to be the first pieces of poetry to break off of the thousand-year-old Persian poetry tradition, almost everyone wrote poetry in what is now considered classical forms. Today many poets of different ages try their hands at writing various forms ranging from the experimental to the primordial sonnet. Their works appear in print in books and magazines as well as online in journals and in innumerable websites and blogs. The advent of Internet in Iran has made possible a more or less democratized access to inexpensive, online publishing outlets, providing many aspiring poets with economically affordable venues to present their works to their audiences. Poetry is omnipresent.

The Iranian literary scene has been witnessing an increase in translated texts from different languages and literatures. The boom began a decade or two ago for reasons not entirely known to me. The result, however, has been a new generation of translators, many of them young, importing works of fiction and poetry, as well as nonfiction and a whole range of academic textbooks. About twenty percent of all titles published in Iran in 2013 have been works of translation.[1] Although it is still not easy to earn a living as a literary translator, at least the translators' names appear on covers and spines, and not in tiny font sizes. Some people buy books based only on the good reputation of the translator. A distinguished translator can be as well known as an established writer. A specialization in translation is also happening in the sense that second-hand translation is being more and more frowned upon. English and French used to be the two main languages from and through which most of world literature found a way into Iran. A heightened awareness of the processes of translation has resulted, among other things, in a predilection, on the part of both the readers and publishers, for translations from the language in which the work was originally written. A retranslation of the works of Chekhov from the original Russian (rather than French) is one example. Another change has been a much more fierce competition to be the first to translate award-winning and popular titles. Award stickers have started to appear on the covers; translators work night and day to finish the latest popular books, such as Harry Potter, before others. Nobel, Booker, Goncourt are names that are being heard and seen on covers more often.

The influx of translated works into the Iranian book market does not, however, seem to have spurred the reverse practice: very few works of Iranian literature are translated into other languages. While the prominent figures of classical Persian literature, such as Rumi and Khayyam, are still the ones most known and published internationally, contemporary works comprise only a negligible portion. One of my goals in starting this project was to contribute to the trickle of translations from Farsi.

The story of this book goes back to when I founded *PARA-GRAPHITI*, an online literary journal that was dedicated, at first, to publishing works of contemporary Iranian fiction and poetry in English. Working on the materials for the journal provided me with an opportunity to familiarize myself and make contact with some younger Iranian poets. I found many good works, some of which found their way into the journal. Before then, I was a writer and translator whose target language was Farsi; that started to change with *PARAGRAPHITI*. The transition was completed when I started the MFA Creative Writing Program at the University of Notre Dame. With the shift in my primary writing language from Farsi to English, I got more interested in translating works of Iranian literature. The idea for this book materialized in Ben Heller's Literary Translation class. For the final project, I translated into English around twenty pages of poetry by a number of contemporary Iranian poets. The fact that the project was well received made me wonder if I could add more pieces to the collection and develop the class project into a book-length manuscript. That's how I started working on the present anthology.

Of the variegated mix of works out there, I was more interested in what the less established were doing, and mostly the youth, the underrepresented of the underrepresented. That's why I set forty as the age limit for the collection. Although one of the poets has recently turned forty-one, at the time of selection and translation, all seven poets were under the age limit I had decided on. I already had a few candidates whose works I was familiar with from *PARAGRAPHITI*; I then went through many online venues reading for poets (men and women alike) to include in the book. My intention was to assemble a rather homogeneous collection of works that would read as a stand-alone book of poetry as opposed to an extensive anthology to include works from all across the spectrum. When I decided which poets would make a coherent ensemble, I read through their works to find the pieces I believed would better lend themselves to translation. While the translations in this book are not meant to be totally domesticized for an English-speaking audience, I refrained from a completely foreignizing translation. I aimed for something in between, something not out-and-out alien, but at the same time, including hints to remind the reader that these are works from another culture across the ocean. One might call it a comfortably foreign translation. Whenever I came across instances in the poems where I was not sure about the text, I would contact the poets (via e-mail and phone) and ask them for clarification. Also, I sought editorial assistance from some fellow poets at the Notre Dame MFA program on some of the translations. We sat together, read the translation in full, and decided on how to render in English certain ideas in the original that might have been hard to grasp for an audience unfamiliar with the Iranian culture.

The poets' relation to the canon was an important factor in selecting the materials for the book. When it comes to translating an underrepresented literature, it might be reasonable to expect to start with the better known. That, however, is not how I went about it. What I did, if anything, is the opposite. Not only are the poets in this collection non-canonical, but some of them were not even published in Iran at the time I was preparing the book. I have always believed that there is a considerable number of quality literary works being produced by those who are not enjoying the spotlight. The editing of this anthology was an attempt to explore a small fragment of the margins of the margins.

A certain number of other factors were also at work in selecting the contents. There were many poems and poets I would have loved to include in this book, but was not able to. Some works included wordplay or cultural and historical references to the extent that I decided I would not able to do justice to the original in my translation. More would have been "lost" than I would have been comfortable with. Those were left out. I should emphasize again that the present book does not have to be taken as a representation of Iranian poetry today. There is much more going on in Iran than I could have summarized in a book. This is a collection of what I deem good poetry by seven younger Iranian poets, one that I hope will shed light on corners of contemporary Iranian poetry less known by others.

—Alireza Taheri Araghi
August 2015

Note

[1] According to http://www.jamejamonline.ir/newspreview/1445810029496864890

I AM A FACE
SYMPATHIZING
WITH YOUR GRIEF

ARASH ALLAHVERDI

Shitkilling

come
come and do drugs
bring the drugs and do it
drink
drink the water
as if semen drink the water

drink and piss
piss on the office ceramic tiles
don't tell your colleague you pissed
tell him this is orange juice
your colleague will cheer up
and say real friends share drinks
and there are consequences
but don't worry
tell lies
sleep
take lorazepam and sleep in the office
think of hips in your sleep
think of the capacities of hips

ponder
ponder and flee
flee into streets and bazaars
climb onto the curb
stand there and sing
sing and say not
say not I know not singing
speak

and eschew the fellowship of the ignoble and the envious maligner
and be never doleful
and rub my compound elixir of lobster dregs and yogurt
and ergot fungi liquids
on your skin
on your penis
on your hands and hips
so their harm won't befall you
and thou shalt live
so you will harm not even an ant
rub
and bend over
shove your mouth into the ant's ear
and utter to him
there are eight paradises
and seven skies and four gates
where art thou now O ant?

the ant crawled into the hole amazed and mysterious
the four angels rush towards you
towards you
to take hold of your four corners
if you don't believe in paradise
and take you to your father-in-law
and then
you will vaguely see
you will see the same ant reclining next to your father-in-law
"son, if there is no paradise, why do you say there are eight
    paradises then," your father-in-law will say laughing

you yourself know you have done drugs
you go and read Marx and Benjamin and Blanchot
you feel like it'll kill you to go to work again tomorrow

and your father-in-law doesn't know you did drugs
you will finally die in the office
you know it yourself
and Bahram knows this too
Ensieh knows this
Feo knows this
Ati knows this
And you understand these things
and you are afraid your jubilant king will never hear the story of
    your perishing

but God himself knows

you also know that God himself knows
and he knows that he himself knows
and he knows that the Lord brings thousands of likenesses
forth
and he himself knows that you
are not even one of these likenesses
and he himself knows that you
are only scum, only excrement
and you yourself know that in excrement
—and the excrement knows it itself—
there are a thousand secrets—swear to God—
not even one is in a thousand roses

and death to the nose
and death to the eye that just won't believe
and death to your childhood
and death to your adolescence and youth
he who has no babe must do school
he who has no money
must get accepted at a public university

must not take up drugs and chicks
must become a respectable person
he knows these things
and he who has money
is no shithead to do school
and be a clerk
and not have a non-cultured chick
and death to his nose
death to his eyes
death to his body
death to his penis
and such are the characteristics of the crowds

climb down from the curb

come and do drugs
come and sniff
and be warned that the nose is not just for dying
come and shit
and fix your eyes on your excrement
zoom in
gaze
and place your excrement on a gold platter
caress it
pick it up and put it on your head
imagine you are bringing me a dowry
imagine you are carrying yourself in your coffin
bring it
bring it so a thousand mysteries I will clarify for you

Tehran is hell
and this will be your fate

this neighborhood is hell
and this will be your fate

come and have sex
have sex
do drugs and have sex
get connected

accept
think
touch
rub
get warm
get wet
have sex

get squished
get shit
get composed
get compressed
this is my most prisoned poem
this is my most poisoned poem
this is my most presumed poem

you are entering my Iranian poem
you are violating my Iranian poem
and this is my own fault
I am born of a slit
I have slit myself from before myself
and I slit everything
and every slit deserves a cock
deserves a cock

deserves a violation
deserves an entry
deserves an employer
and this
is my right

climb down from the curb hateful excrement
come let's go do drugs
come
God's guarding us
come

Anger

I open the window
stick my head out
and spit on the passersby below
(Second Floor, Apt. 4)
people ring the bell
throw stones
I don't open
I'm afraid
I'm shivering

I wish I hadn't spit
I wish I hadn't opened the window
I crawl under the blanket and wail
I pee

smash smash ...

but no one hears
the house under the blanket is cold
everyone's blood is cold
Mother won't clean up the shards
on purpose as always
now the people are gone
on purpose as always
and you don't give a shit
while I wonder
          in my dolorous lonesomeness
what to do with my future spits?
my family laugh:

"stop thinking
you fuck up when you think
get out
work's what makes a man a man"[1]

but you think you can mess with me?
I open the window again
stick my head out
I'm ablaze
I'm shining
the cars down there pull a bluff
they hit the brakes
          "There he is, it's him."

they throw stones again, rascals
I spit
I dance and spit
suddenly the divine wind blows
and carries my spit towards them
and by God's wrath
the earth swallows them with their cars
but
the survivors jump on me
it wasn't me
it was the wind, swear to God
stop hitting
let me go
this is God's work:
he created the wind
          the water
          the earth
          and me

me who will slay my enemies
since they all
have conspired
to pass under my bedroom window
        indifferently.

so
spit on your graves
under my bedroom window!

God is still at work creating the world
and you don't give a fuck
and you, you do not give a flying fuck
I want to sleep

good night, my illegitimate love
good night

Bleeding

there is blood coming
blood
is
coming
blood is coming with a stranger
blood is coming in a cab
blood is coming with a loose woman
the loose woman and the blood are approaching my eye
I stare at the voluminous member of the blood
blood whispers to the woman
the loose woman bends into my eyes and forces her breast
      her nipple
into my mouth
blood takes the loose woman's hand
and drags
and takes her away
his head emerges from between my mouth and teeth
slimy
the woman and blood go home
his body dripping with my saliva
blood comes out
blood is something between shame and fury
blood sends the loose woman home in a taxi
blood looks at me
I soil myself
blood pinches his nose
and rushes out of his eyes

blood drips on his own face
blood wipes his face
blood looks in the mirror
          "It's just blood" he tells himself
I realize the loose woman hasn't been able to satisfy our blood
blood sits
exerts himself
wrinkles his eyes and forehead
brings out blood
and holds a drop of himself in his hand
a drop that turns into "another blood"
another kin blood
blood and "another kin blood" go into my room

blood sticks his head out of the door
          I mean our own good friend blood
and approaches my eyes and says open your eyes a little, moron
the intellectual blood, his pressure goes up
leaves the blood
blood is throwing up
blood
the blood of madness
goes back in again
keeps his cool
and buries himself in blood's warm arms
as if blood is taking it

his sound is coming
it's as if blood is taking a shit
as if blood is dying giving birth
no

it becomes silent
as if blood gets well
blood is putting on his pants
gets out of the house
with "another blood" who has his pants already on
bloods who get out of the house
bloods who get out of the house
bloods who look out of the house

bloods who take the subway
bloods who mistake someone for Walter Benjamin on the subway
bloods who stick to Walter Benjamin
bloods who watch the ads
bloods who have been robbed on the subway
bloods who have gone to the police station and said Walter Benjamin
    have robbed them
bloods of madness
bloods of philosophy
bloods of depression
bloods of unemployment
bloods of indifference
bloods of anemia

little
less
I have dreamed these
I know nothing else

blood
is coming alone
blood is coming on foot
blood his head is spinning

I hold him in my arms
blood implores closer and closer to my eyes
I bend over
and he drinks blood from my breast
blood is going
blood
is
going
blood
is
going   from here

Decay

I am turning into an onion, sweetie!
this is clear
I'm sorry
that my feet, my socks, my pants, and my shoes are getting sucked
    into my bottom.
I'm so sorry
I liked those socks very much, especially those wool knee-high
    socks I bought last year with Ati at Haft-e Tir Square
I'm sorry
time has no doubt come
for my arms and my face
I'm proudly turning into a big fat onion
a fistful of beautiful concentric circles
a foul-smelling big fatty in whose foul smell there is divine
    wisdom dormant
this impending incident however
is definitely not a divine incident or event
this incident
is a ruling
a ruling issued against me by a judge at a Greater Tehran District
    Court
this ruling
is acceptable unquestionably
this ruling
is a game
a definite game
is definitive
the message got down to us crystal clear
I accept it

I'm ready
because I have no more interest in my limbs
because I have no more interest in my head and face and mouth
because the sun will never shine on me again
just as the snow
just as the rain
just as the blizzard and hail
just as the spring.

it's late
I should hurry
vein to skin
listen up
today is the day of killing
today is Thursday whereas tomorrow is Thursday
ergo
today is Thursday evening
this is what my room's desert tells me
this is what someone, a familiar voice, from my room's desert tells me
a little sand is blowing with the wind
everywhere is full of lights and sparks
everywhere is bright and windy
sand
sand
sand all over my body sand
all my hair
all my eyelashes sand
I will never see you
make a sound
talk to me a little
talk to me more

why don't you believe my words then?
someone on the desert hills of my room talks to me every day
it was he who told me
You are turning into an onion, son
and you are aware that an onion is a being and the essence
of every being is its soul and you will turn into an onion
undoubtedly
I'm sorry, son
I'm sorry

the voice didn't last
        left unseen
nothing's left

"God gracious is left
God immaculate
God beautiful
God of speech
God of murmur
God of wrath"[1]

To Halve

it started
it started to halve
the it-started-to-halve poem started
the start was halved
a mouse snuck under my shoes
the mouse was halved
my feet were halved
I glanced at my watch
time was halved
light and dark was halved
my pain was mostly worse
most of my pain was halved
half of my pain was mostly worse
it was eating my body
my body was halved
I fell asleep from pain
my sleep was halved
I flopped onto the wind
the wind was halved
a wind carried my half onto the roof
a wind carried my other half down to the sea
the sea and the roof were halved
the house and the fish were halved
the sleeping room was halved
the waking room was halved
the door was halved
the seafloor was halved
I got out of the door
my getting out was halved

the ships were halved
the passengers were halved
Enqelab Square was halved
the drownings were halved
the mermaid was halved
men and women were halved
the breasts and thighs of the drowned were halved
the drowning sea came to an end
and I was halved more
and landed in several places

landing
descending
falling
and happiness
happiness was halved
misery
was halved
office work hours were halved
joy poured down half of my throat
my consciousness was halved
my unconsciousness was halved
childhood was halved
I went home
my home and family were halved
my father was halved
my mother was halved
my brother was halved
my wife was halved
I returned from pain
my pain returned
my return was halved

the news came to the bed
I saw half of me was not there
half of my other half was not there either
I needed it no more
there was blood
I was scared
the bed was halved
my fear was halved
my words were halved
tongue was halved
poetry was halved
future was halved
everydayness   night   despair   immigration   and   hope
all were halved
earning bread was halved
lies and grief were halved
separation was halved
and the halves were separated more
one of the halves went longer   went further
one of the halves stayed   stayed
and my pain got mostly worse
I shed tears
my tears were halved
I wiped my face on my sleeve
my face was halved   was halved more
and dropped down on the ground
and the earth was halved
and everything sank into its creases
and finished

the finish was halved
and halving

was finished
was finished
was finished

About the Poet

ARASH ALLAHVERDI hails from Shiraz. He started writing poetry at the age of fifteen. He has mostly published his poetry in electronic formats and online. His second book, *The Book of Blood*, failed to receive publishing license and so was published as an e-book. He has a master's degree in the Economics of Art and currently works as a branch manager at Iran Language Institute.

Notes

Shitkilling
> Coedited with Thade Correa.
> First published in *Asymptote* and *Tripwire*.

Anger
> [1] This line is an allusion to the second hemistich of the first line of a poem by Iranian poet Mohammad Taqi Bahar (1884–1951). The poem was taught in the Farsi Literature textbook in the fourth grade in the eighties. It's an anecdotal narration of how a wise old man's dying words become a lesson for his sons to learn the value of work.

Bleeding
> Coedited with Drew Kalbach
> First published in *PARAGRAPHITI*.

Decay
> First published in *Tripwire*.
> [1] These words are from a speech the esteemed Iranian writer, Houshang Golshiri, delivered at Mohammad Mokhtari's funeral.

SODÉH NEGINTAJ

Have You Thanked Yourself

do you remember yourself?
Saturday Shahrivar the third[1] with stiff knees
sprawled in patient clothing
with Nars
with Samira
with a few others who shone flashlights at the golden stall by the
   Hemmat Highway
with your long-gone-dead suffering that passed you by on a
   motorbike
with your friend's dead head stuck in the hinge of the car
was laughing and was nothing
but a funny hand light in the hand of another dead
that made-happy
that defective miss
flung into the scraps of moon and visits and turkey stew
that lonesome sweetheart
with a treasure of grasses and glasses
that flashing signal light that was swollen in the bed and
   remembered you
you soared and remembered it
Ana Ana Ana
have you thanked yourself
and the house from the Saljuqi era that pissed in a chest
      skinnier and skinnier and skinnier
and the trembling that flung you from terrace to terrace and from
   there to another and from there to another
lavender and green and sometimes even white
and who the fuck do you think you really are
but the roar after a Barcelona game

but continual late payment notices
and an eye in which there was nothing but dusty metal
and nothing
and really nothing
do you even remember me
cute and dumbass, with a neck longer than the galaxy
standing in front of Sadi Hospital with legs and arms and
    shoulders and ass
smoking and laughing on the trunk of your car with seven sequins
    in my neck
saying, I'll crawl to Sadi in August and be back
what do you even remember except the tree and the sky and your
    pain
who do you even remember except the creaking of that door that
    opened and closed opened and closed opened and closed
do you remember me, as if you were sunk in an ugly swivel chair
    barking orders
get my pills
get my dentures
get a handful of storks and stars
get the rope
get the lighter
get my keys
get my chocolate
get my bugle
get my glamor
get my wings
get my fighter
get my grave
go now go go go
go and leave the door ajar

It's Nothing

should upside-down stand
should by-prior-appointment stand
should extraordinary, like a ballerina on tiptoe, stand in front of you
should ordinary, like misery, very ordinary, stand in front of you
should the crushing of thousands of workers' fingers in the wheels of
    industry stand in front of you
should oppression stand in front of you
should the swinging of a woman's arms and legs every night with the
    intention of throwing her on the asylum bed stand in front of you
should wrapped-in-the-sheets, wrapped-in-chocolate, with a bloody
    mouth among washers of the dead and juice boxes and camphor
    stand in front of you
should Bin Laden with a hole in his head in a six-bed bedroom stand
    in front of you
should the Middle East casualties stand in front of you
should the sun in his new pajamas stand in front of you
should your empty account on the ATM screen stand in front of you
should three thousand shitty images of the houses you rented stand
    in front of you
should all the landlords of the city stand in front of you
should the real estate brokers of Ma'ali Abad / Eram / Atlasi / Zerehi
    / even Airport Square stand in front of you
should Shiraz stand in front of you
should missed calls from all the meat-eaters / plant-eaters / man-
    eaters / angels / flying-things / crawling-things / predatory-things /
    jumping-things / photos / dishes / dresses / even Prince of England
    stand in front of you
should Nars's trembling voice at the end of the line stand in front of
    you

should
> your forged documents
> your forged poems
> your forged this
> your forged that
>> stand in front of you

should your vain migrations stand in front of you

should Café Jeanne d'Arc and the hasty smoking of your last
friend stand in front of you

should Peyman's math graphs in your every fall stand in front of
you

should your unfinished tasks stand in front of you

should the mild earthquakes in your temples stand in front of you

should objects left from your last paycheck stand in front of you

should your lost states of mind stand in front of you

should the "colorful-eyed" people from the Soltaniyeh Complex
who won't pull it out of their family friends stand in front of
you

should all of Sadra's loves stand, blossoms-in-hand and successful,
in front of you

should Irancell's[1] welcome tune stand in front of you

should the Internet speed like an ancient, groomed horse stand in
front of you

should the Lake's charlatans' shorts stand in front of you

should acting-freak, auteur-freak, canary-freak wusses stand in
front of you

should the inscrutable brown sky

putrid staircases of all government organizations stand in front of
you

even the friendship comedy

the friend with three lanterns on his head and three goat horns in
his eye

the friend who leaps through a hoop into your arms–squeaking
who leaps from your arms onto Facebook–squeaking
who leaps from Facebook into the next hoop–squeaking
who leaps through the next hoop into your arms–squeaking
glorious, ripped, outrageous
squeaking and circular
should the repeating of friendships stand in front of you
should the pristine moments of befuddlement stand in front of
   you
should
        the bullshitting fascist
        the bullshitting ruler
        the bullshitting boss
        the bullshitting intellectual
        the bullshitting citizen
        the bullshitting doctor
            stand in front of you
should the new symptoms of the cured disease and its
   unsubsidized costs stand in front of you
should atrophied muscles of the clock hands stand in front of you
should fucked-up art, fucked-up mind, fucked-up dream, fucked-
   up act, fucked-up homeland, fucked-up language, fucked-
   up poem, fucked-up stomach, fucked-up body, fucked-up
   generation stand in front of you
should you stand in front of you
should you throw up between two fingers
two antlers
two teeth
two thighs
two breasts
two shooting stars asleep on a cloud
should you gush onto stars and carcasses

onto nervous signs
should you gush onto ooh-la-la things
ooh-la-la metamorphoses
ooh-la-la biographies
ooh-la-la speeches
ooh-la-la losses
ooh-la-la traumas
ooh-la-la censorship
ooh-la-la bras
ooh-la-la broodings
ooh-la-la falls
ooh-la-la fears
ooh-la-la laws
ooh-la-la brawls
ooh-la-la leopard dresses
ooh-la-la truths
ooh-la-la ass kissers
ooh-la-la hairstyles
ooh-la-la graves
ooh-la-la pains
ooh-la-la virgins
ooh-la-la footsteps
ooh-la-la winters
ooh-la-la spruces
ooh-la-la trees
ooh-la-la sunsets
ooh-la-la deaths
ooh-la-la things
ooh-la-la things
ooh-la-la things
ooh-la-la things
the world is an ooh-la-la metaphor   it stands in front of you

the missing photos are metaphors
this is it
this is laughter
with fine punctured wings hanging from its tail
                          it's nothing   standing in front of me

And Should You Feign Resistance

you are holding the slide from behind and you think you are
     holding your mother from behind
and your suitcase
your nail polish
your crimson sleep mask
the bus ticket
all
you have left them all
you are gone
tagging along behind you are the professors of fatal phobiology
     with cleft breasts beneath their clothes
formal breasts
breasts halted in wool cloaks
those two dear silly queens
and meanwhile a woman with a bullet in her head is walking with
     someone in Virginia
talking non-stop of Shiraz sour orange orchards
and should you see old bachelor Rock boys playing in their hope-
     hole basements
and the choir, tucked into the wall, boom-booming you away
this is terrifying
this is terrible
you never even dreamed you'd slouch for hours
and exert yourself like a stag for hours
low for hours
smoke cheap crap
pull this and that person's hair
in the pavement / in the wound / in the office bric-a-brac
should you drag your velvet love on your shoulders with all of

this and all sorts of other things for a hundred and fifty-eight
    long days
should you drag firmly and hard
and say oh my love / my Xanax love / my three-headed, tailed
    love
the world is fucked up / Iran is fucked up / my shoulder is fucked
    up
and say jump up my love / jump down my love / jump up onto
    the clouds my love / jump my love
and should you make a move in the double-pane window, in the
    sickness of things, in the hall of the flesh and feign resistance
and cry along Sattar-Khan[1] and back
again cry along Sattar-Khan and back
and see a thousand scattered eyes rolling along Sattar-Khan and
    back
and see yourself
hiding behind the stall sticking out your snout
telling the gendarmes, someone was on his way to his father's
    mansion, he went instead to the Milky Way
and you continue:
magic? magic is to lie in the grave and not die of loneliness
to slip into new creatures and snitch from beyond them
magic is to witness the exploded stomachs in Naser Khosrow[2] and
    still feign resistance
and to see a shabby branch of a tree that's feigning resistance itself
and to be dying to be among the disappointed Maracanã[3] crowd
to go to Sarvenaz[4] Alley and go down there
to go to Birds Garden
to go to the final word of creation
and then to go to the last scene of *Mouchette*[5] and call out to the
    wagoner
why not?

Circle of Elephants

look there
where set the moon, the stars, and the sheep
at a wave of the hand
a long hand hanging from Austrian sequins
with seams patterned like onions and seashell
where souls leave the poem to collect empty shell casings
everything works hand in hand so a heart might go
clanking away
for a visit
all you need is for things to work hand in hand
or some things at least
the heart slumps and a halo hangs from its waist
to fuse poetry and mouth and lantern at a high altitude
look at the four camels smoking pipes in the sky
look at the birds in the Birds Garden
standing placard-in-hand in front of placardless people
look at the food and sickness and stand in front of Evin Prison
hold the spoon under your breast like a sword
and behold the glamor in gold teeth and fake hearts
step down a long corridor and sleep with a woman
and look at your eyes sweating in the sleeves of a deer
someone is there who is sinking in the island of the beard
neighing in an apricot tart
pissing street after street in heavenly domains without giving up
spin and see your heart among the bottles
back there
by the circle of elephants in the forest of spindly legs

Take Shelter in the Forest of White Rocks

on that day
let me sit you there
on the whirlpool of fog and pillows
on the shadow of the silkworms
right under the green coat rack
beside that shitty nostalgia
where bubbles of love march into your mouth and keep going
in spite of the sunshine
in spite of basic preferences
in spite of the clerks who hide their monthly breakfast in the drawer
and land on papers
let me sink my grudging hands into your head
grab you between my tears
let me excite you
in the gigantic doors of the wardrobe
you chubby
you almost-happy freckled mystery
hanging from the street lamp and sand ribbon
covered in blossoms on the neck and thighs
take shelter in the forest of white rocks
with those massive confused hands of yours
lie on the wooden bridge
with that woman
upside down by a tree
lie on the tin chest of Jesus
on the mouths of the ghosts and spirits or thereabouts
I will love you anyway
the day when you will have rested your chin on your hands
with your crumpled face simple and unique

I will write of you
ramble on for three pages
        that you have worn a strange look
        that your eyes are bent hinges
        and your shoulders are a roller that starts in sleep
        rolling and fucking the skies, the stars, the clouds
        and your hands that swell
isn't it splendid?
I meant to say light but I hit the panes
that day
close to paradise
over deaths and doohickeys
so much that befall us
so much that there is
        between thoughts and laughs

Miming

disgusting stars stare at you
when you're cheating
   hungry in your white clothes
when you place your brother in the hole
   lovingly with Jasper stones
the magicians of the proper looks investigate you
and drive their thin antennas into your flesh
you sink into ice to recognize your true self from behind the mask
as if they imagine you lonely and aloof
none of the ones they take is like you
none of the ones they throw into holes is like you
none of the ones they hug in the streets is like you
   the ones who have not been crumbled under electric shocks
   who still have shaking stars in their pockets
blank screens pass before you and you become all those who have
 cried on your shoulders and none was like you
but it was your brother who cried in the basement and rubbed
 himself against the lead wall
it was your brother onto whose wounded eyelids you flung
 yourself
but the stars will never understand that following your vice you
 were flung
   towards the bodies
   towards noxious and valid things
they shove a big pipe down your lungs so you'd murmur your
 aliases into creatures
with sad powdered eyes in the mime show
so you'd shove your useless bandaged hands into your body and
 perish on the flooring

what will become of the things that will be left
even your anal skin tag
and your eyes that piss on the sky tiredly every night
and finish their job
and only finish their job
then pull their pants up
so you'd welcome everything with bandaged hands and a white
    dress

About the Poet

SODÉH NEGINTAJ is from Shiraz. She is a poet and translator. Her book of poetry, *Sepasgozari kardei az khodat aya* [*Have You Thanked Youself*] has been published by H&S Media. She studied Mechanical Engineering and Urban Design and is currently a college instructor. She lives in Shiraz.

Notes

Have You Thanked Yourself
> Coedited with Drew Kalbach.
> First published in *PARAGRAPHITI*.
> [1] August 25.

It's Nothing
> Coedited with Thade Correa.
> First published in *Hayden's Ferry Review*.
> [1] Iran's second largest telecommunication company.

And Should You Feign Resistance
> First published in *Asymptote*.
> [1] A street in Tehran and also in Shiraz named after one of the central figures in the Iranian Constitutional Revolution who is considered by many Iranians as a national hero.
> [2] A street in Tehran, notorious for being a center where rare types of medicine could be found, often at high prices. Shady characters lingering in the street could be sellers of medicine. Fake and expired products getting passed off as the original by the dealers in this street is not unheard of.
> [3] Maracanã is the largest stadium in the world. As many as 199,854 gathered to watch the 1950 World Cup final match.

All Brazil needed was to score one more goal. The disappoint-
ed crowd left the stadium after Uruguay won the game 2–1.
[Note by the poet.]

[4] An Iranian girl's name.

[5] *Mouchette*, Robert Bresson, 1967. [Note by the poet.]

BABAK KHOSHJAN

Arena

as if it's Iraq's Seventh Division   in the left side of my head
as if it's Iran's corps   *trample trample* in the right side
of my head

and in the middle of the arena
the old rag-and-bone man
under all that smoke and fire
is dipping bread
in his bowl of yogurt soup
a military march playing on the loudspeakers
mortar shells whistling indifferently
and Dad's too much a scatterbrain to see the warning signs
Dad dances with a Bouncing Betty[1]
and I lose all my childhood
Mom's voice booms from the bedroom
"shut that damn thing up!"

as if a clothes line   in the right side of my head
as if the cotton beater   *twang twang* in the left side
of my head

and in the middle of the yard
Mom is plunging me in dirty washbasin water
stomping with rolled-up pant legs
the cotton beater beats   *twang twang, twang twang*
and my dad's cotton beard floats in the air
a red alert siren is on
"Dear listeners"   *trample trample*
they shelter me in the basement
I pound my fist on the door

"I won't do it again! On grandma's grave!"

as if the jury   in the right side of my head
as if the reporters' cameras   *click click* in the left side of
                                          my head

in the middle of the court
Jean-Paul Sartre with that curling white wig of his
bangs the gavel to say
"Man is condemned to be free"
Dad in the guise of my public defender nags
"I'm just looking for an honest man"
my eyes are half-closed from the white flashes of light
"Get up, boy, it's almost noon," says Mom
drawing the curtain

as if it's not the executioner   in the right side of my head
as if it's not the waiting crowd   cheering in the left side of
                                          my head

in the middle of the arena
I am tied to a horizontal stake
Dear listeners
this is the white alert siren
and what it means is that the narrator of this poem
is now standing on a platform
on which all problems will be erased
this is the white alert siren
you may now leave your shelters
this is the white alert siren
you can come out of your shells
this is the white alert siren

So That Minotaur

If my ear could capture the all the sounds of the world, I should hear his steps. I hope he will take me to a place with fewer galleries and fewer doors. What will my redeemer be like?, I ask myself. Will he be a bull or a man? Will he perhaps be a bull with the face of a man? Or will he be like me? ...

"Would you believe it, Ariadne?" said Theseus. "The Minotaur scarcely defended himself."

—Borges, "The House of Asterion," Translated by James E. Irby [1]

my mother
she withered
and they bestowed my childhood
      to a cow's udder
so that now I am
      foster-brother to all the calves in the city
so that I am a bull
so that I am a man
so that I am an illegitimate child of mancow
so that I am lowing today
      here in the thousand twists
        of this plaza
so that I'm goring
      the heartless walls of the now
so that the earth was on my horns from the beginning
when my neck snapped
they put the earth down

my father
he reared up

my mother's breasts
                breaths
                cravings
had not withered yet
when she threw me up under the feet of the crowd
                at Shahyad Square [2]

so that now time
                caught on my horn
                                —as if the ring of a yo-yo string—
                                                orbits my head
                swinging
                                away
                                                and
                                back
so that I become a child like myself
                do homework
so that I get beaten
                for my bad handwriting
so that I rebel
                like my mother
so that I go to war
                like my father
so that I blister from mustard gas
                like my brother
so that I become Yahya
                hang myself from a beam
                                in the chicken farm
so that once again
so that a hundred times again
                I become a bull like myself

school
university
factory
home
dairy farm
kindergarten
school
Shahyad Square
dairy farm

my wife
she withered
and I bestowed my daughter's childhood
  to a cow's udder
so that she'd be foster-sister to her father
  now she's a woman
  she's a cow
  she's a woman
    illegitimate child of mancowman
  keeps lowing
  goring
    my nasal septum hole
  kicking the rusty ring
    in my nasal septum hole
it hurts
since the time
  Father tied to it
    a rope
      the other end of which
      was noosed around
      the neck of the statue

  dragging me

     —I think next time the yo-yo revolves
       it should be called Freedom—
  under the feet of the crowd in the Square
     to topple the statute
it hurts
   my nasal septum hole
it hurts
   the knot on the ring
     in my nasal septum hole
it hurts
   even the mark on the neck of the statue
      from the noose of the rope
        the other end of which
          was tied to the ring
           on my nasal septum hole
   in the square
     —I couldn't read the name
      on this circle of the yo-yo—
it hurts
   the marks from my father's horns
   the marks from my daughter's kicks
   the marks from my own hoof-strokes on me

I saw me
in the mirror
and realized
   I was first a bull
     then a man
I stood on two legs
and realized
   I was first a man
     then a bull

that I have been listening for the footsteps of Theseus
who knows well
> how painful it is to be a manbull
that my being a bull prevents me
> from being a man
that my being a man prevents me
> from being a bull
that I have wallowed around
> till the cows come home
>> in the foolish twists of my father's brain
that I have limped
> till the cows come home
>> under the blind tramplings of my daughter's vanity
that I have become apples
> till the cows come home
>> between the teeth-grinding of my mother's cravings
that I have become a bull
> till the cows come home
>> in the abominable lowing of my own vertigos
Swear to God
that I know
that cows will point their fingers at me
that if he is not back
> before dusk
on the next circle
I'll pierce my daughter's nasal septum

Theseus
> where are you stuck, boy

under which fold of this thousand-fold labyrinth
> fallen under Ariadne's foul flirtings
>> is he stuck

that

    it's getting dark

that

    my mother
    is withering again

that

    it is getting late

Proposal in Azadi Street

when the song of the mourning dove
landed on your windowsill
the odds were four-to-one against us, Lady
       with your Qajari Coffee [1]
            one to dying young
            three to a slow death

when the song of the mourning dove
shattered on your windowsill
we were fallen
       sprawled in the street
and the old female possum
memorized the smell of our body
       with her long snout
hard-headedly
we stared into the eyes of the possum
whose every hair
was a ravenous viper
that had traded its beauty
with grimy filthy immortality
and a slow death

we
       the last survivors of the masterless samurai
had our heads in the basin pan
while twelve rugged knights
       around the table
broke bread and drank wine
to their master's health

with a stupid stubbornness
we tried to remember our name
we
             surrounded by twelve rugged knights
             in the feast of bread and wine
             in the basin pan
             in our blood
tried to remember our name
Lady was a prefix for your name
we wanted to remember our name
but all we remembered was
we stared in your eyes
             so long
                         we turned into stone
we got so close to your breasts
that we fell
             breathless
                         on barren rocks
                         somewhere in Icaria
we ran our hands over the scent of your body
so much that our odds
             one-to-four
died young

we tried to remember our name
but all we remembered
was that our name was something
like the song of a mourning dove
that
             landed
                         and shattered
                                     on your windowsill
Lady of Qajari Coffees!

Miracle

these days
I am thinking of an old crumpled snake
whose coils
were tattooed on the back of
a young and lithe dancer
       years ago
I feel sorry for him
that he can't even shed
his historical coils
through looks so lewd
       and gazes so rude

these days
I am thinking a lot
about the poor elephants in the Abraha and Ababil tale[1]
about the unfortunate horses in Pharaoh's army and the
   devouring of the Red Sea[2]
about people,
      step
          step
             step
               to God,
               Chogha Zanbil Ziggurat[3]
about van Gogh's sunflowers
Ray-Ban sunglasses
cataracts
      boy, you think way too much
      you'll start thinking things
the call for morning prayer means

go to sleep, heathen
God only knows
maybe in his next life
this old snake will turn
into an arrow-pierced tattoo
on the hairy arm of the Caspian
miracles come in all shapes

A Poem for You

your eyes [*]

---

[*] The warmth of your lips
the passion in your arms
the calm of your shoulders
and even the delicateness
of your hands
have been censored from
the frankness of this poem
due to the meanness
of public morals.

About the Poet

BABAK KHOSHJAN is a poet, scholar, and critic. He served as the editor of *Vazna* online literary journal for two years. He has two books of poetry yet unpublished. He studied philosophy and currently lives in Tehran. References to social, historical, and sometimes mythical issues are abundant in his poetry.

Notes

Arena
> Coedited with Thade Correa.
> First published in *PARAGRAPHITI*.
> [1] A type of land mine that, when triggered, launches into the air before exploding at about the waist level.

So That Minotaur
> Coedited with Jayme Russell.
> First published in *Modern Poetry in Translation*.
> [1] Jorge Luis Borges, *Labyrinths: Selected Stories and Other Writings* (New Directions, 2007), 140.
> [2] Azadi (literally, "freedom") Square, in Tehran, is Iran's second largest square (after Naqsh-e Jahan in Isfahan). It is where the monumental Azadi Tower is located. Before 1979, the place was called Shahyad Square.

Proposal in Azadi Street
> [1] The Qajar Dynasty ruled Iran from 1794 to 1925. Qajari Coffee refers to the political execution method favored by a number of Qajar Kings. The victim was invited to the court and offered a cup of poisoned coffee. In case he would refrain

from drinking from the cup voluntarily, he would be forced to drink the cyanide-contaminated potion.

Miracle

[1] (In Quranic tales) Commanding an army riding elephants, Abraha sets out to destroy Kaaba. In defense, a flock of Ababils is sent by God. The birds drop on Abraha's elephants and men tiny clumps of dirt that demolish the army of the ambitious king.

[2] (In Quranic tales) In an attempt to flee Pharaoh's army, Moses and his people come to the Red Sea (or the Nile). Moses throws his cane at the water. The waters divide, opening a path for the prophet to cross. After the last of Moses' followers step out of the seafloor, the waters flow back, drowning Pharaoh and his army.

[3] Chogha Zanbil is an ancient Elamite complex in the Khuzestan province of Iran. It is one of the few existent ziggurats outside of Mesopotamia. (*Wikipedia*)

ALI KARBASI

The Story of the Man Who Didn't Have Dirt to Bury His Lion

the lion who
looked after me
for years
looked after me in his free time
looked after me in the forest
slept by my head at night
the lion whose mane
I blow-dried
in the evening
the lion who
made me loveable by
and for ...

my lion
died of wounds
that would never heal

"Ah," loudly he said
with a smile
narrow like an Indian's,
"Goodbye my friend
Goodbye"[1]
and then
died
and then I
tried to
throw some dirt
on my dead lion's body
tried to

keep a fire alight
at his grave
for a little while
tried to plant a few flowers at least
but
there was no fire
there was no flower
and no dirt
there was nothing there
because my lion
was dead

De la Guerra

don't be sad, my son
you too will one day
have a mustache
and muscles
and no horse
will have the balls to kick you

don't be sad, my son
you too will one day
have a rifle
sit atop your horse
and girls in poofy colorful skirts
will bring you water

don't be sad, my son
you too will sweat
you too will triumph
you will get drunk
you will laugh

don't be sad
don't mind this bloody wound
like a dimple on the face
these wounds
are passed
from father to son

Burning Steaks & Ribs

you will never see
the world's worst fire
mustard
is a big explosion
that little by little
in the hospital ...

—Extra mustard, sir?
—No, thanks.
—Extra mustard, ma'am?
—No, thanks.

they look you over
they sway away

—Extra mustard, sir?
—No, thanks.
—Extra mustard, ma'am?
—No, thanks.

in the desert
we have two brown bodies
and twenty orange people
scream
scream

the hill is laden
with bodies
down there
the enemy folks
are launching a strike
over there
Haji is going to shower
further away
Reza
is homesick
again

Tick Tock   Tick Tock   Tick Tock
Tick Tock   Draraaaaahhh[1]

truth is
my dear
your slab of rock
       ripped apart
          my waterfall

truth is
ma'am
the cogwheels of your watch
          ripped apart
            the insects of my emotions

and your Jeeps
       ripped apart
         my Vietnamese legs
            from both sides

your bomb
burned my children

my poem
ran to me
on the road
stark naked

truth is
ma'am
you
attacked

by air and land
with heinous clusters
of napalm
and bursts of
machine gun fire
but
where are you taking my body?
with all due respect
where are you taking the body, bitch?

Yo-yo

if
I were a tired giant
if I were a tired giant
sleeping in the sun
in the factory yard
you would need a crane
to move me
if I were a bigger giant
about twenty tons
you would need a tower crane
to move me
I'm a small giant
of water
a tower crane is not enough
bring a bowl
or I'll evaporate
into a giant
of cloud
and rain
on the roof of your warehouse

cliffs don't dream
cliffs
duplicate
the same dream
night after night

whores
never have sex

cliffs
are in love
with whores

Cliffs, Fairies, and Men

one day I will come home rowing
"Wow, you're back early"
you will say, surprised
"I was away catching fish for you my dear wife"
I will say
and you will be happy

one day I will come rowing
along the shore
along the twisting line of your hair
I will dock in between your breasts
your fisherman
is a half-owl
very attentive
with eyes so sad
I hear
"… sometimes cliffs and fairies … people"

one day I had come rowing
Troy was small
Helen's breasts were small
I saw her picture myself

one stormy day
I came home quietly
my home was empty
the police
had seized
the satellite dish

I'm worried about gas
the car is almost out of gas

one day I came home
you had dyed your hair
green
again
a nice wind was blowing
the birds
couldn't help
screeching

when I came home
a bird
was perching
on the shore

the moon
is an unhappy ass
the sea
is a poet
who has taken it too far
the ducks
have taken flight towards the cliffs
cliffs are not afraid of the waves

the yellow seals
came from the sea
with machine guns
with
twirled mustaches
dragging
themselves
rasping
towards
us
on marble derrieres
with fine hair on their bodies
and a gentle dripping
of water and of cold
but
they came from the sea
with mustaches
with machine guns
the sun was shining
the storm was pounding
and we were still
proud of
the sound of waves
breaking on cliffs
in our headphones

the wind blew
dropped a lentil
into the alley
the alley pondered
and remembered
  a lentil tree is not possible
at night
the lentil on the blacktop
at noon
the lentil on the blacktop

tick tock
tick tock
it's night
and you are
guarding your loneliness

a tank is a nonchalant creature
pays no heed to anti-personnel mines
pays no heed to soldiers' legs
pays no heed to rivers
or hills
or trenches

it goes
and goes
and goes
then stops suddenly
thinks a little

and says
"boom"

I slept in my trench
I said prayers in my trench
I killed my enemy in my trench
when I returned
the home was as always
same orange bricks
same old bed
same plain pajamas
no matter how much I fought at home
no matter how much I slept at home
no matter how much I said prayers
you never came back from LA[1]

whores
there are tons of them
from the Vietnamese side
from the Thai side
white
simple
sad
with plain handkerchiefs
for crying
for leaving behind
for wiping the machine guns

burly bikers
have taken my bunny
to the desert
my bunny
was broad-shouldered
had stopped eating carrots
had even
a shotgun
my bunny
with shoulders broad
is gone

his wooden home
is still
in the yard

About the Poet

ALI KARBASI is an amateur Iranian poet, blogger, and short story writer. His work often employs black comedy, parody, romance and satire. He enjoys using or combining materials from American pop culture to Old Persian mythology. He's got a master's degree in Electrical Engineering from Wright State University in Dayton, Ohio. His publications consist of limited writings in journals and anthologies.

His obsession with dark satire and eroticism limits his chances of having a decent publisher or a writing career in Iran. Therefore he works as an engineer at a steel factory and publishes most of his poems and writings online.

Notes

The Story of the Man Who Didn't
Have Dirt to Bury His Lion
    First published in *PARAGRAPHITI*.
    [1] The same English words appear in the original quote, transcribed in Farsi script. Quotation marks exist in the original.

De la Guerra
    "De la Guerra" is the original title in Roman letters.

Tick Tock   Tick Tock   Tick Tock
Tick Tock   Draraaaaahhh
    [1] About twenty-three, -four years ago, there was a daily show on the Iranian national radio called, literally, "The Calendar of History." The host would read, in short vignettes, very brief accounts of the most important events that had happened on

that specific day throughout history. Each vignette started with the phrase "X years ago today…" The theme music of the show was an excerpt from Pink Floyd's "Time." The clip started after the chiming of bells fades away and the beating starts. The title of the poem alludes to the radio show and Pink Floyd's "Time" as its theme music.

Yo-yo
  First published in *Bat City Review*.

[the yellow seals]
  First published in *Bat City Review*.

[I slept in my trench]
  [1] "LA" is written in the English alphabet in the original.

MAHNAZ YOUSEFI

Rasht

remember now your heavy accent, Rasht
remember now our bodies drenched in the rain
that blew their tops at night
remember now your green hands
that are of that stinky gray ilk
no memorial left after the city
from Family Hospital[1] we arrived at Razi Hospital
with a fistful of veins and swallowed pills
with a woman in labor, with honking and pain as always

hey Rasht!
with that heavy traffic near your anus
stray dogs won't understand your drivers' sleepless nights
truth is, Rasht, truth is
when coupled cousins killed themselves in a family feud
we had an eye for Siyahkal and Lahijan and other cities too
we remembered Resalat Street
and the ambulance now far from this damned place
destroyed in vain by family distances
city in vain with your four seasons suspended in rain
truth is, we never belonged to you

no memorial left after you
the pungent scents of Zarjoob[2]
the pungent scents of the bazaar
we are afraid of mother's breasts that smelled of the fish seller
we are afraid, Rasht
many a wolf[3] sniffs at you
"wolf" was the paradoxical identity of your writer too

had a distant relationship with the deceased
but wouldn't cease
and what can make you know what men ended up deceased
oh, what men!
with all striped clothes in Lakan [4]
with every other sorry face of theirs behind the bars
and what can make you know what crucial role the airport played
like inflamed buttons of a sick breast
with everlasting cancer and instinct and nature
and what can make you know what it means that nature was blue
    at times
you are alone with sands
you are alone with kites
hey Rasht, you were the North and yet you did not have a sea,
    Rasht
did not have a sea, Rasht
did not have a sea ...

poor Father
just that he planted Mozhdehi [5] in your godforsaken place
poor Father
just that because of you he was unmanly
though he was a standing man
just that he is standing on Sepid River [6]
with a hanging tongue and a tail out of sight
just that he is standing with his back to Tehran
with a bone in the tooth and a bruised howl
poor Father
just that he didn't know your map looks like the head and neck of
    a lonely dog
just that forlorn
just that mapless

just that citizenless
just that we are a few drags heavier than you
you can still   Ali
you can still   Hasan
Mitra   Soheil   Hooman   Farzam
you can still   the neighbor's kids
Emad and Samira
you can still   Saeed who was lonely in this damn place
only if there were a memorial left of you so we could pray for you
only if you knew that nature was Lahijan which was high at times
you should say *hani* instead of *hande*
you should say *tara* instead of *tebe*[7]
and use no verb other than fuck
—How long is Amin taking shelter in your fucking place?
you,
stared, stoned
withdrew with your anus

Amin was silent ...

so many names names
just that we crave names no more names
with you nothing to do, Rasht
with anyone else nothing to do, Rasht
just that we have nothing to do we take to tension
just that we take to tension we have nothing to do
my dearest Rasht!
with that ilk of yours sucking off the breast
with the drinking struggle in the mouth
with a couple of glasses of milk after the suicide pills
we roamed through your pharmacies night and day
and every time we were out of antidepressants

we took to contraceptives
and every time we were done
we were pregnant
we are afraid of postpartum depression
you tell us you tell us what to do what to do with the orphanage
    we have in our wombs
you tell us you tell us what to do with the blood clots clots
boy's bulging arms
girl's full breasts
and bits and bits and bits of fetus pouring out of your threshold
who was home alone?
who was hugging their knees
crying into the cuffs of their sleeve?
who in the darkness was
the destiny of the gloves in the closet?
who was it that announced the international blood day
when we returned—mature—
from the apartment bathroom to your streets
too afraid to tell mother
about the below-the-belt pains
in the first unfinished municipal pothole?
who was it that walked in you friendless?
only if there were a memorial left of you so we could pray for you
and then come back with our back
to the bona fide madmen of the bazaar
back to the bona fide madmen
back
to the bona fide madmen
no memorial left of the city
no memorial left of the city
no memorial left of the city
no memorial left of the city

no memorial left of the city
no memorial left of the city

...

in Chamkhaleh[1]
there is no cemetery
            that hasn't buried you, Ali
in Chamkhaleh
winter perished
            perished
                        in every star, Ali
and in every hospital
the neurology ward
            had been already stolen, Ali
and you thought a sickness was
            within the power of the soul
and pain within your eccentric family

your being is not better than your not being
and you're not being is not better
            than anything else

limping
limping
in the weeks to come I found my new face
      limping
chanting
       the women come
               go
with forbidden breasts, brimful with drinkable alphabet
and your lips,
      oh luscious moment of writing
your lips had swallowed their words
before I came back home in their echo
their lips had swallowed my echo

their yards became tall buildings
intruding Mother's scarflessness in our yard
and gave birth to the flowerbed
      that we had never sown
these I shouldn't know
      but I have learned them
I have known none
unhappier than you
      you the luscious of writing

oh fat! so fat!

no one believes I grieved
my body contrary to my thin veins
these I shouldn't know

but I have grieved them
they emptied their small canteens
        of me
so I would be left alone
        at school
        at home
how lonely our flowerpot has become at home
how in vain you gave birth, Mother
how in vain you gave birth!
praise in the tight white swaddling
praise in the white of every snowflake
praise in the winter
        the summer
                the four seasons that depress the ceiling fan
we slammed the oppression onto the street
directed our eyes at the cab driver
        at the passengers in the back
                at the window
we directed our eye at the side mirrors
"objects in mirror are closer than they appear"
our bride
        more beautiful in the mirror
offered condolences to the mirror
when Mother greeted her
        with the blood from the sacrifice

oh fat! so fat!

no one believes I'm a bride
white dress contrary to my loose heart
contrary to you
        you luscious moment!

when you were away I took the pen

for *water*

for *father* [1]

they revolutioned me on the walls

when you were away they stuck their fingers down my throat:

woman!

woman!

and the woman who had a good throat threw it all up

when you were away,

I went away

I came back

their tongues sealed my chest

from the house came sounds of pregnancy

again

sounds of Noah and Kenan history

again

they moved us in books every day

in thin veins and loose hearts

the silence dies every day

the child whose drawings were

bride

bride

bride

got married

and me

who never colored anything

will be buried between a white stone and black dirt

every day I'm either awake

or my eyes are always silent

my lips are always silent

the word is not a good time for me not to love

may it be
         for me
                  new schools
let my name
         be written
                  in new letters

oh fat! so fat!

no one believes it's me

in me a hand
in me an eye
in me is a face that loses its smiliness with the seasons
of us   of us
a party   a birthday
pounding till the incident at dawn
smile, you unhappy barefoot!
left in the stairs was nothing but my footsteps
how much for this gray cell that eats
                              eats the thought?
how much for this trashing trash can full of writing?

in debt, we slid our hands
                    into our pockets
mother
father
a family has judged my chagrin
and me
        I suffer the world only as much as my womb
and my baby will come
                my baby
                        who is the memory of a justice
and his face
        his face
                will beam in an annual routine
how much for it?
my hand
        this is it
my eye

            this is it
I am a face
            sympathizing with your grief

Dogs Got Back to the Streets

a few white splotches depart the sky for us
not different from a few white swans departing the sky
a few white swans depart the sky for us
       even when not different from white splotches
not different from a few black crows departing the sky
when only white splotches depart the sky for us

it always starts again
it always starts   it's always four years   it starts
                         always

becomes eight years
it always starts   it's four years   becomes eight years
                         always

the forward event
the rearward event
the side-view-mirror event
the your-brakes-have-failed-won't-you-get-out-and-holler-with-us
   event
the bend-down-your-head event   won't-you-empty-your-bowels-
   with-us event
the upward event
slowly
slowly
towards the sky
the like-a-raindrop-bullet event
even when
     from the sky
        a few black crows
           for us
             fare

—What's the fare to Siyahkal?

Is He [not best] who responds   to the desperate every moment
    all night and day?
Is He [not best] who responds   to the desperate every moment
    all night and day?

all night and day   always all night and day
always flung towards the sky at a certain hour of the dusk
lying among the crowds in the backstreets of a married woman's eyelids
a few married streets with white residents
even when my brothers
        with bloodshot eyes
my brothers
        during whose escape   the sound of their ears are here
        during whose escape   the smell of their noses are here
        during whose escape   the taste of their mouths are here
here
        dogs with bowed-down heads
here
a robe fled from the short-term memory
        sprawled over large bodies
        with large blisters
right during the most seasonal sensitivities of the Jungle Movement[1]
the bridling of the anger of a downward bullet
        under the itching of the gullet
right under the folds of fat under the throat
there is war abreast of the throat
the war between the foot and the large genital sores
my beloved home and the large genital sores
my beloved and the large genital sores
genital sores and genital sores

there's a war
there's been a war for four years
there's been a war for eight years
foam oozing out of the mouth of the sky
the earth covering its ears with its hands

man of adventure
kiss the adventure
           on the mouth
kiss the human being
           with a spoon in hand
           and weak white powders
kiss it
           the little play of the tongues   with long kisses

to the sinuous sneezes of the white jungle
white
white
white
white

About the Poet

MAHNAZ YOUSEFI is the writer of *Tasliyat be zan* [*Condolences to the Woman*]. She is from Rasht, a city north of Iran, by the Caspian Sea. She is interested in Gilaki literature and history and tries to create images that are ethnic and local and deal with issues that rise from the juxtaposition of the local vs the central. She thinks her awareness of the Gilaki language improves her poetry. She believes the way she tackles with the language in her poems will suffer in translation unless she is as proficient in a second language as her mother tongue to translate her poetry herself. She exploits language, imagination, and history to explore modern life. She has a second manuscript, "Dogs Got Back to the Streets," ready for publication. She is a law school graduate.

Notes

Rasht

Coedited by Thade Correa.

First published in *PARAGRAPHITI*.

[1] A maternity hospital in Rasht. [Note by the poet.]

[2] Zarjoob is a river in Rasht, also a neighborhood by the banks of it. Zarjoob is one of the two branches of Sepid (Persian for "white") River.

[3] [Originally *varg*,] Means "wolf" in the Gilaki language. Also a Gilaki writer's pen name. [Note by the poet.]

[4] A village in Gilan Province, Iran.

[5] An orphanage in Rasht. [Note by the poet.]

[6] Second longest river in Iran. It flows through Rasht and meets the Caspian Sea.

[7] *Hani* (West Gilan) or *hande* (East Gilan) means "again," and *tara* (West Gilan) or *tebe* (East Gilan) means "for you." [Note by the poet.]

[in Chamkhaleh]
¹ Chamkhaleh was a village in the Gilan Province, Iran. At the 2006 census, its population was 1,814, in 510 families. It was merged into the city of Chaf and Chamkhaleh. (*Wikipedia*)

[limping]
¹ The very first two words first-graders are taught to write are "water" and "father." Both are among the simplest Farsi words consisting only of the first two letters of the alphabet: *ab* (/ôb/) for "water," and *baba* (/bŏbŏ/) for "father/dad."

Dogs Got Back to the Streets
¹ The Jangal (Jungle) Movement, in Gilan, was a rebellion against the monarchist rule of the Qajar central government of Iran. It lasted from 1914 to 1921. (*Wikipedia*)

SHAHRAM SHAHIDI

Peace After Cigarette Butt Storm

it's good enough that a bullet
isn't coming
death is wounded and now
before it comes
I can sit in the trench
and light a cigarette

There Was a Shadow Sitting
in the Trench's Cup

a violet has grown
     on the Corporal's body
a wind has blown
     on the dryness of the lips of the soldiers of the regiment
                                  that got wiped out

the corporal is lying
     in the shade of the tank
          fingering a rosary

it will end
it will not end
it will end
it will not end

Leave Me Your Teeth

the colonel was hungry
dinner was still being fixed on the enemy's map
burned soldiers
and crispy bread
and a bowl that smelled like dung

Apocalypse Now

when Israfil blows the horn
I will just go to sleep
the world will be quiet
there will be no more soldiers to fight

Two Sides of a Coin

I was the full half of the war
and the other half
a soldier standing with a loaded gun
pissing on my luck
      or in his pants from fear

a little to the right
a little to the left
the treasure is right here
my bones and those of
a thousand and one others who fell
bury us a little

my eyelids   wintry
your bra   summery
how deep my sleep
how lonely your heart
and photos
and laughs

blood
drips from my cheeks
it's a cold winter
with no snow
with no you

unless she hears
a rocket whistle
my wife can't sleep
her sore eyes won't rest

the soldier brought home hell
hid it in his bedroom
Are you back?
     his mother asked
and the soldier leaned his head
     on his mother's shoulder
          forever

A War for All Seasons

the corporal was rainy like spring
the colonel was cold like winter
the Iraqi captive
        sweated like summer
the soldiers fell like fall

Blood Rain

rain in Faw[1]
Faw in rain
bullets and tears
        raining
rain in the eyes of a woman holding a framed photo
photo of a woman stuck out of a uniform pocket in the trench
                         in the rain
the sound of falling
      in the drainpipes
      in the trenches
      in the sky
          where lightning rumbled
a far-off light flickered in the rain
the corporal trickled with
            blood
            tears
            and rain
onto the ground where his daughter was buried

Faw was rainy
it poured down
      from Baghdad
      from clouds
         that smelled like mushrooms

he meant to rise   he fell
that's how war is, you know?

bite the enemy soldier
if he tastes sweet
he is a drafted loser, too

Your Mediterranean Warms Me

every other dress button of yours
do ... undo
and do my eyes open to the warm Mediterranean of yours
Damascus is sitting on your two brown tacks
when the wind blows
the turmoil of your white dress leads its streets to disturbance
       in a muggy afternoon

I have counted buttons
that hide your summer afternoon nakedness
       from the Cairo of my eyes

you become Beirut when you jump up to the sound of crows that
caw caw
       and the news
           hanging
              in the air
                 is a man they are killing in Kahrizak

it's all in the papers:

Bab al-Azizia Walls Still Afraid of Dogs
Bu Sa'id Clouds Get to My Homeland Tomorrow

last button of your dress ... will get undone in Tehran

About the Poet

SHAHRAM SHAHIDI is a satirist, poet, and fiction writer. He writes columns in a number of Iranian newspapers and magazines. His poetry has appeared in three anthologies, and his short stories won him two honorable mentions in national contests. His collection of short stories, *Deer Sleep with Eyes Open*, was published in 2010. He currently lives in Tehran and works as a civil engineer.

Notes

Peace after Cigarette Butt Storm
> Coedited with Thade Correa.
> First published in the April, 2014 issue of *RHINO*, and winner of the 2014 *RHINO* Poetry Translation Award.

There Was a Shadow Sitting in the Trench's Cup
> Coedited with Thade Correa.

Leave Me Your Teeth
> Coedited with Thade Correa.

Apocalypse Now
> Coedited with Thade Correa.

Two Sides of a Coin
> Coedited with Thade Correa.

Blood Rain
> [1] "The Faw Peninsula is a marshy region adjoining the Persian Gulf in the extreme southeast of Iraq, between and to the

southeast of the cities of Basra (Iraq) and Abadan (Iran)....
During the Iran–Iraq War in the 1980s, al-Faw was bitterly
contested due to its strategic location." (*Wikipedia*)

Your Mediterranean Warms Me
　　Coedited with Jayme Russell.
　　First published in *PARAGRAPHITI*.

AHOORA GOUDARZI

Kill Bill

(Volumes One and Two)
Directed by Quentin Tarantino

These poems are dedicated to Taimaz Afsari

El Paso Chapel

MY HEROINE
How did you find me?

BILL
I'm the man.

that dress didn't look good on you, my heroine
heroines don't marry
heroines get killed on their wedding day

now think of the bullet
the bullet that put you to sleep
the bite that woke you up
the baby that's not in your womb
now let's move half of your body
let's try to move your fingers
now let's Kill Bill

O-Ren Ishii
Matsumoto

stay under the bed
and think of the sword
that your father's chest will sheathe
the sword that is now in front of you
I know
your world is not animated
maybe if I saw your world as you do
I would hate the hattori hanzo sword
only if you forgot the smell of your mother's blood
only if
you were
never
under the bed
at that
moment

Nikki

MY HEROINE
It was not my intention to do this in front
of you. For that, I'm sorry. But you can
take my word for it. Your mother had it
coming.

sheathe your eyes, my daughter
try not to smell your mother's blood
sheathe your eyes, my daughter
try not to smell vengeance
think about it, maybe you are not the heroine
think about it, maybe
you'll become O-Ren Ishii
anyway when you grow up
if you still feel bad about my heroine
even if she is not around
I'll be waiting for you

Hattori Hanzo, a Man from Okinawa

```
HATTORI HANZO
Revenge is never a straight line.
It's a forest.
```

do not breathe his name
let the fog on the window shout the name out
then decide
craft your last sword
and bear in mind
your sword will not Kill Bill
bear in mind
that my heroine
will wipe clean with her sleeve
the name you left on the window

Confrontation in the House of Blue Leaves

O-REN
You may not be able to fight like a samurai …
but you can at least die like a samurai.

MY HEROINE
Attack me … with everything you have.

if you don't sheathe your sword
if you close your eyes and open the door
if you sink your feet in the snow
if you press your feet so hard
the snow seeps from between your toes
you will be a leaf with a drawn sword
let loose your ocher yellow onto the snow
paint the snow ocher
let fresh blood stream
let the story flow

now even if you sheathe your sword
you'll still be my heroine
you'll still Kill Bill

Budd, Bill's Brother

BUDD
That woman … deserves her revenge.
And … we deserve to die.

step out of the car
light the lighter
not your cigarette
let's glance up the rocks
go to your trailer
sit on a chair facing the door
load your gun
leave the lights on
and let's take a look further down the story

further down the story
my heroine will open this door
and you will have two options, Budd
pull the trigger
let blood splash in your face
bury my heroine
to fertilize the earth
until the Black Mamba kills you
not pull the trigger
and take pride in getting killed
by my heroine's Hattori Hanzo sword
further down the story
you will have two options, Budd

Master Mei

```
MASTER MEI
It's  the  wood  that  should  fear  your
hand … not  the  other  way  around.
```

your cruel trainings
I know them, Master Mei
you owned my heroine's hand
the coffin cracked
a white lotus
sprouted
from between my heroine's fingers
your cruel trainings
I know them, Master Mei
but
you
do not know the glamor of crying
after revenge

The Grave of Paula Schultz

BUDD
Now you're going underground tonight,
and that's all there is to it. But,
when I bury ya, I was gonna bury you
with this.

let dirt be thrown on this coffin
let it be that you wake up
to find yourself buried
then open your eyes
and calm yourself down
let the past remember you
let your fingers aim the right spot

the earth is a stricter mother, my heroine
try to come out of the womb
try hard so the earth won't abort her child

Elle Driver

no heart will
break for you
pity you
miss you
you saw your world through a narrow hole
when your pupils
were so wide
they could embrace
a white lotus
Master Mei
pulled out your eye
and you
eclipsed in your gloom
now my heroine
is squishing your other eye under her foot
and you're dead meat
Elle
struggling in your quagmire
my heroine will open the door
leave the room
and the door
will close itself on you

Bill

```
BILL
How do I look?

MY HEROINE
You look ready.
```

in the eyes of my heroine
see a cathedral, Bill
that smells of blood
see a silent piano
a bullet that won't kill
a bullet that will revive my heroine
now in the eyes of my heroine
you can see yourself, Bill
a man who doesn't have but
five more steps to death
now you can take steps
one at a time
so that in your heart
the white lotus
may open its petals
one at a time
one, the wind will blow into your flute
two, my heroine will choke up
three, my heroine's fingers will shake
four, silence will flow into the flute
five, tears will fall on the table

About the Poet

AHOORA GOUDARZI is the writer of the book of poetry, *The Third Narrator* [*ravi- e sevvom*]. His second book, forthcoming from Cheshmeh Publications, is titled *Kill Bill*. Two chapters of the book are inspired by Quentin Tarantino's *Kill Bill* and Robert Rodriguez's *Sin City*. In them the poet makes conceptual connections between the historical and political situations of Iran and the two movies by thematically reproducing them in the form of poetry. He has published a number of essays on poetry and cinema and served on the editorial board of *Vazna Journal*.

Acknowledgments

My sincerest gratitude goes to Johannes Göransson who was a great help in the different stages of this project.

I would like to thank Ben Heller whose Literary Translation class was where the idea for this book originated.

I am grateful to Drew Kalbach, Thade Correa, and Jayme Russell who helped me edit some of the poems in this anthology.

Thanks also to my fellow Notre Dame MFA students in Johannes Göransson's Translation Workshop who read parts of the manuscript and made useful comments: Peter Twal, Sarah Roth, Jessica Newman, Jayme Russell, Jace Brittain, Paul Cunningham, Rachel Zavecks, Thirii Myint, and Alice Ladrick. I am grateful also to my other Notre Dame friends who helped me with my random questions (such as "What's the difference between "dirt," "soil," and "earth"?"), especially Katie Lattari and Beth Towle.

And finally, I would like to express my gratitude to the editors of the journals that published poems from this book.

About the Editor and Translator

ALIREZA TAHERI ARAGHI is an Iranian writer and translator. His translations have appeared in *Asymptote*, *Hayden's Ferry Review*, *Tripwire*, *RHINO*, and *Bat City Review*, and his translation of Shahram Shahidi's "Peace Before Cigarette Butt Storm" won the 2014 *RHINO* Translation Prize. His fiction has appeared in the *Gloom Cupboard*, *Green Mountains Review*, *Notre Dame Review*, *Rusty Toque*, *Re:Visions*, and *Avatar Review*. He holds an MFA in creative writing from the University of Notre Dame and edits the online journal *PARAGRAPHITI*.